The Path to Financial Freedom: Mastering Money Management and Building Wealth

By Tyler McQuade

The Path to Financial Freedom: Mastering Money Management and Building Wealth

Contents

Introduction 6
   Purpose of the Book 6
   What You'll Learn 6
   The Importance of Financial Literacy 7
Part 1: Building a Strong Financial Foundation 8
   Chapter 1: Understanding Your Financial Health 8
      Assessing Income, Expenses, and Debt 8
      Calculating Net Worth and Setting Financial Goals 9
   Chapter 2: Budgeting Basics 10
      The 50/30/20 Rule and Other Budgeting Methods 10
      Tools and Apps for Tracking Expenses 11
      How to Avoid Lifestyle Inflation 12
   Chapter 3: Eliminating Debt 12
      Types of Debt: Good vs. Bad 12
      Strategies for Paying Off Debt: Snowball vs. Avalanche Methods 13
      Avoiding Future Debt Traps 14
   Chapter 4: Building an Emergency Fund 15
      Why It's Essential and How Much You Need 15
      Steps to Save Consistently 16
      Where to Store Your Emergency Fund 16
Part 2: Growing Your Wealth Through Smart Investing 17
   Chapter 5: Investment Basics 17
      Understanding Risk and Return 17
      Types of Investments: Stocks, Bonds, Mutual Funds, ETFs 17

The Path to Financial Freedom: Mastering Money Management and Building Wealth

Compound Interest and the Time Value of Money 18
Chapter 6: Retirement Planning 19
    Why You Should Start Early.. 19
    401(k)s, IRAs, and Other Retirement Accounts 20
    Estimating Your Retirement Needs................................. 20
Chapter 7: Diversifying Your Portfolio 21
    The Importance of Asset Allocation................................ 21
    How to Balance Risk and Reward 22
    Strategies for Long-Term Growth................................... 22
Chapter 8: Investing in Real Estate.................................... 23
    Rental Properties, REITs, and House Hacking 23
    Pros and Cons of Real Estate Investment 23
    Steps to Get Started... 24
Chapter 9: Navigating Cryptocurrency 24
    What is Cryptocurrency? 24
    How to Invest Wisely in Digital Assets 26
Part 3: Creating Passive Income Streams 26
Chapter 10: The Concept of Passive Income 26
    What It Is and Why It's Powerful 26
    Active Income vs. Passive Income.................................. 27
Chapter 11: Online Business Ventures............................... 28
    Blogging, eBooks, and Affiliate Marketing 28
    Starting a Dropshipping or E-Commerce Store 29
    Leveraging Social Media for Profit................................. 30
Chapter 12: Investing in Dividend Stocks 30
    How Dividends Work 30
    Building a Portfolio of Dividend-Paying Stocks.............. 31

The Path to Financial Freedom: Mastering Money Management and Building Wealth

Chapter 13: Peer-to-Peer Lending and Crowdfunding 31
    How Peer-to-Peer (P2P) Lending Works 31
    Risks and Returns 32
    Platforms to Consider...32
Chapter 14: Monetizing Your Skills 33
    Creating Online Courses..33
    Freelancing and Consulting 33
    Turning Hobbies into Income Streams 34
Part 4: Achieving Financial Independence 34
Chapter 15: The FIRE Movement 34
    What is Financial Independence, Retire Early (FIRE)?....34
    Different Types of FIRE: Lean, Fat, and Barista 35
    Steps to Achieve FIRE 36
Chapter 16: Tax Optimization Strategies.........................37
    Understanding Tax Brackets and Deductions..................37
    Tax-Advantaged Accounts...37
    Reducing Your Tax Burden Legally 38
Chapter 17: Frugality and Mindful Spending......................39
    Living Below Your Means..39
    The Difference Between Needs and Wants.....................39
    Finding Joy in Simplicity...40
Chapter 18: Staying Motivated on Your Financial Journey ..40
    Tracking Progress Toward Goals......................................40
    Dealing with Setbacks 41
    Celebrating Milestones..41
Conclusion and Next Steps 42
    Recap of Key Takeaways..42

The Path to Financial Freedom: Mastering Money Management and Building Wealth

 How to Start Implementing Strategies Today 45
 Encouragement for the Journey Ahead 48
Appendices and Resources...49
 Glossary of Financial Terms..49

The Path to Financial Freedom: Mastering Money Management and Building Wealth

Introduction

Purpose of the Book

In today's fast-paced and ever-changing world, personal finance has become an essential life skill. With rising living costs, increasing debt levels, and the growing complexity of financial systems, managing money effectively is more critical than ever. Yet, financial literacy remains a significant challenge for many people, leaving them unprepared to make informed decisions about their finances.

This book is designed to bridge that gap, empowering readers to take control of their financial future. Whether you're just starting your journey toward financial independence or looking to refine your existing strategies, this guide will provide the tools, knowledge, and confidence you need to succeed. From mastering the basics of budgeting to exploring advanced investment opportunities, every chapter is crafted to help you build a solid financial foundation and achieve your long-term goals.

What You'll Learn

Throughout this book, you'll discover practical strategies and actionable insights to transform your financial life. Key topics include:

1. **Budgeting:** Learn how to create a realistic and sustainable budget that aligns with your goals and values. Discover tools and techniques to track your spending, save consistently, and avoid common pitfalls like lifestyle inflation.

The Path to Financial Freedom: Mastering Money Management and Building Wealth

2. **Investing:** Explore the world of investments, from stocks and bonds to real estate and cryptocurrency. Understand how to build a diversified portfolio, balance risk and reward, and grow your wealth over time.

3. **Passive Income Strategies:** Unlock the secrets to generating income streams that require minimal effort once established. From dividend stocks and rental properties to online businesses, you'll learn how to create financial freedom through passive income.

4. **Achieving Financial Independence:** Discover the principles of the FIRE (Financial Independence, Retire Early) movement and how you can tailor these strategies to your unique circumstances. Learn to live below your means, optimize your taxes, and design a life centered around your priorities.

By the end of this book, you'll have a comprehensive understanding of personal finance and the confidence to make decisions that align with your financial goals.

The Importance of Financial Literacy

Despite its importance, financial literacy is often overlooked in traditional education systems. Many people graduate with advanced knowledge in subjects like history or calculus but lack the basic skills needed to manage a budget, understand credit, or plan for retirement. This lack of knowledge can lead to costly mistakes, such as accumulating unnecessary debt, failing to invest, or living paycheck to paycheck.

The Path to Financial Freedom: Mastering Money Management and Building Wealth

One of the most pervasive myths about money is that you need to be wealthy to start building wealth. In reality, financial success is about making consistent, informed choices over time. This book will challenge misconceptions like "investing is only for the rich" or "budgeting is restrictive," showing you that anyone can achieve financial stability with the right mindset and tools.

Another common misconception is that personal finance is overly complicated or requires advanced mathematical skills. While the financial world can seem intimidating, the core principles are simple and accessible to everyone. This book breaks down complex topics into easy-to-understand concepts, ensuring that readers from all backgrounds can benefit.

Ultimately, financial literacy is about empowerment. It's about understanding your options, making informed decisions, and taking proactive steps to secure your future. By committing to this journey, you're not just improving your financial situation you're gaining the freedom to live life on your terms.

Part 1: Building a Strong Financial Foundation

Chapter 1: Understanding Your Financial Health

Assessing Income, Expenses, and Debt

Before you can build a strong financial foundation, it's essential to understand where you currently stand. Assessing your income, expenses, and debt gives you a clear snapshot of your financial health.

1. **Income:**
   Start by listing all sources of income, including

The Path to Financial Freedom: Mastering Money Management and Building Wealth

your salary, freelance work, investments, or any other streams of revenue. Be sure to account for both regular and irregular income, such as bonuses or side jobs.

2. **Expenses:**
   Track your monthly expenses by categorizing them into fixed (e.g., rent, utilities, insurance) and variable (e.g., groceries, entertainment, discretionary spending). This will help you identify areas where you can cut back and optimize your spending.

3. **Debt:**
   List all of your outstanding debts, including credit cards, student loans, mortgages, and personal loans. Note the interest rates, monthly payments, and total outstanding amounts. Understanding the total debt load and the cost of servicing it is key to making informed financial decisions.

Calculating Net Worth and Setting Financial Goals

Once you've assessed your income, expenses, and debt, you can calculate your net worth, which is a critical indicator of your financial health.

1. **Net Worth Calculation:**
   - **Assets:** List all your assets, including savings, investments, property, and any other valuable possessions.
   - **Liabilities:** Subtract your liabilities (e.g., loans, credit card debt) from your assets.

- **Net Worth Formula:** Net Worth = Assets − Liabilities

A positive net worth means you own more than you owe, while a negative net worth indicates you owe more than you own.

2. **Setting Financial Goals:**
   Based on your financial assessment, set realistic short-term and long-term financial goals. These could include paying off debt, saving for retirement, buying a home, or building an emergency fund. Use the SMART criteria (Specific, Measurable, Achievable, Relevant, Time-bound) to make your goals clear and actionable.

Chapter 2: Budgeting Basics

The 50/30/20 Rule and Other Budgeting Methods

Budgeting is the cornerstone of managing your finances effectively. Several budgeting methods can help you allocate your income wisely, but the 50/30/20 rule is one of the simplest and most popular.

1. **50/30/20 Rule:**
   This rule divides your after-tax income into three categories:
   - **50% Needs:** Allocate 50% of your income to essential expenses such as housing, utilities, transportation, and groceries.

The Path to Financial Freedom: Mastering Money Management and Building Wealth

- **30% Wants:** Spend 30% on discretionary expenses like dining out, entertainment, and hobbies.
- **20% Savings & Debt Repayment:** Dedicate 20% to saving for the future and paying off debt. This could include retirement savings, emergency fund contributions, and loan repayments.

2. **Other Budgeting Methods:**

    - **Zero-Based Budgeting:** Every dollar is assigned a job, whether it's for expenses, savings, or debt repayment. At the end of the month, your budget should balance to zero.
    - **Envelope System:** Cash is allocated to envelopes for specific spending categories (e.g., groceries, entertainment). Once the envelope is empty, no more money is spent in that category for the month.

Tools and Apps for Tracking Expenses

There are several tools and apps available to help you track your expenses and stick to your budget.

1. **Mint:** Tracks your spending, categorizes transactions, and offers insights into your financial habits.
2. **YNAB (You Need a Budget):** Helps you allocate funds to specific categories and prioritize savings and debt repayment.

3. **EveryDollar:** A simple budgeting app that follows the zero-based budgeting method.
4. **Personal Capital:** Tracks both your spending and investments, helping you see a complete picture of your financial health.

How to Avoid Lifestyle Inflation

Lifestyle inflation occurs when your spending increases as your income rises. To avoid this pitfall, it's essential to remain mindful of your financial goals.

1. **Live Below Your Means:** Resist the urge to upgrade your lifestyle every time you receive a raise or bonus. Instead, allocate the extra money toward savings, investments, or debt repayment.
2. **Prioritize Financial Goals:** Focus on long-term goals like building wealth and achieving financial independence rather than indulging in short-term pleasures.
3. **Automate Savings:** Set up automatic transfers to your savings and investment accounts, ensuring that you prioritize your future before spending on discretionary items.

Chapter 3: Eliminating Debt

Types of Debt: Good vs. Bad

Not all debt is created equal. Understanding the difference between good and bad debt can help you make better financial decisions.

The Path to Financial Freedom: Mastering Money Management and Building Wealth

1. **Good Debt:**
   Good debt is an investment that will likely increase in value over time or help you generate income. Examples include:
   - o **Mortgage debt** (if it's for a home that appreciates in value).
   - o **Student loans** (if they lead to a higher-paying job).
   - o **Business loans** (if they help you grow a profitable business).

2. **Bad Debt:**
   Bad debt is debt that doesn't provide a return or has high interest rates. Examples include:
   - o **Credit card debt** (due to high interest rates).
   - o **Personal loans** (for non-essential items or experiences).
   - o **Car loans** (for depreciating assets).

Strategies for Paying Off Debt: Snowball vs. Avalanche Methods

There are two popular methods for paying off debt: the **snowball method** and the **avalanche method**.

1. **Snowball Method:**
   - o Focus on paying off the smallest debt first while making minimum payments on larger debts. Once the smallest debt is paid off, move to the next smallest. This method

provides psychological motivation as you see your debts disappearing.

2. **Avalanche Method:**
   - Focus on paying off the debt with the highest interest rate first while making minimum payments on the others. This method saves you more money in interest over time, but it may take longer to see progress.

Avoiding Future Debt Traps

To avoid falling back into debt, consider these strategies:

1. **Build an Emergency Fund:** This will help you cover unexpected expenses without resorting to credit cards or loans.

2. **Use Credit Wisely:** Pay off your credit card balances in full each month to avoid interest charges. Only borrow for things that appreciate in value or help you earn more money.

3. **Live Within Your Means:** Stick to your budget and avoid impulse purchases that could lead to unnecessary debt.

The Path to Financial Freedom: Mastering Money Management and Building Wealth

Chapter 4: Building an Emergency Fund

Why It's Essential and How Much You Need

An emergency fund is a financial safety net that helps you cover unexpected expenses without going into debt. It's essential for financial stability and peace of mind.

1. **Why It's Essential:**

    - **Unexpected Expenses:** Medical emergencies, car repairs, or home maintenance can happen at any time. An emergency fund ensures you can handle these without relying on credit.

    - **Job Loss:** If you lose your job or experience a reduction in income, an emergency fund can help you maintain your lifestyle while you search for new employment.

    - **Peace of Mind:** Knowing that you have funds available for emergencies reduces financial stress and allows you to focus on long-term goals.

2. **How Much You Need:**
   Financial experts recommend saving between **3 to 6 months' worth of living expenses**. If you have dependents or a less stable income, aim for the higher end of that range.

The Path to Financial Freedom: Mastering Money Management and Building Wealth

Steps to Save Consistently

1. **Automate Savings:** Set up automatic transfers from your checking account to your emergency fund account each month.

2. **Start Small:** Begin with a small, achievable goal (e.g., $500) and gradually increase your savings as you can.

3. **Cut Back on Non-Essential Spending:** Review your budget and find areas where you can cut back to contribute more to your emergency fund.

Where to Store Your Emergency Fund

1. **High-Yield Savings Account:** Look for an account with a competitive interest rate to help your emergency fund grow over time.

2. **Money Market Account:** These accounts often offer higher interest rates than savings accounts and are a safe place for your emergency fund.

3. **Avoid Investing:** While investing offers higher returns, it also carries risk. Keep your emergency fund in a low-risk, easily accessible account.

The Path to Financial Freedom: Mastering Money Management and Building Wealth

Part 2: Growing Your Wealth Through Smart Investing

Chapter 5: Investment Basics

Understanding Risk and Return

Investment is about balancing risk and return. Understanding these two concepts is crucial for making informed decisions.

1. **Risk:**
   Risk refers to the possibility that an investment will not perform as expected. This could mean losing money, not earning the expected return, or the value of the investment fluctuating. Different types of investments carry varying levels of risk. Stocks are generally considered higher risk compared to bonds, for example.

2. **Return:**
   Return is the profit you make from an investment. It is typically expressed as a percentage of the initial investment. Return can come in the form of capital gains (increase in value), dividends (income from stocks), or interest (income from bonds).

3. **Risk-Return Tradeoff:**
   In general, higher potential returns come with higher risk. It's essential to assess your risk tolerance and investment goals to find a balance that suits your financial situation.

Types of Investments: Stocks, Bonds, Mutual Funds, ETFs

There are several types of investments, each with its own risk profile and potential for return.

The Path to Financial Freedom: Mastering Money Management and Building Wealth

1. **Stocks:**
   Stocks represent ownership in a company. When you buy a stock, you're buying a small piece of that company. Stocks have the potential for high returns, but they also come with higher risk due to market volatility.

2. **Bonds:**
   Bonds are essentially loans that you make to governments or corporations. In exchange for your loan, you receive periodic interest payments, and the principal is returned when the bond matures. Bonds are generally considered lower risk than stocks but offer lower returns.

3. **Mutual Funds:**
   Mutual funds pool money from many investors to invest in a diversified portfolio of stocks, bonds, or other assets. They provide diversification and professional management but often come with management fees.

4. **ETFs (Exchange-Traded Funds):**
   ETFs are similar to mutual funds but trade like stocks on the stock exchange. They offer diversification and low fees and can be a good option for investors looking to minimize risk.

Compound Interest and the Time Value of Money

One of the most powerful concepts in investing is compound interest, which allows your investments to grow exponentially over time.

1. **Compound Interest:**
   Compound interest occurs when the interest earned

on an investment is reinvested, so that in the next period, interest is earned on both the initial principal and the previously earned interest. This leads to exponential growth.

2. **Time Value of Money:**
   The time value of money refers to the concept that money today is worth more than the same amount of money in the future due to its potential earning capacity. The longer you invest, the more your money can grow through compound interest.

Chapter 6: Retirement Planning

Why You Should Start Early

Starting your retirement savings early is one of the most effective ways to ensure a comfortable retirement. The earlier you start, the more time your money has to grow through compound interest.

1. **Power of Compound Interest:**
   Starting early allows you to take advantage of compound interest over many years, which can significantly increase the amount of money you accumulate for retirement.

2. **Time to Recover from Market Downturns:**
   The earlier you start, the more time you have to recover from market fluctuations. Even if there are periods of loss, a long investment horizon allows you to ride out these downturns and recover.

401(k)s, IRAs, and Other Retirement Accounts

There are several types of retirement accounts that offer tax advantages, which can help you save more for retirement.

1. **401(k):**
   A 401(k) is an employer-sponsored retirement plan that allows you to contribute pre-tax income, which reduces your taxable income. Many employers also offer a match, meaning they contribute additional funds to your 401(k) based on your contributions.

2. **IRA (Individual Retirement Account):**
   An IRA is a personal retirement account that offers tax advantages. There are two main types:
   - **Traditional IRA:** Contributions are tax-deductible, but withdrawals are taxed.
   - **Roth IRA:** Contributions are made with after-tax income, but withdrawals are tax-free.

3. **Other Retirement Accounts:**
   - **SEP IRA:** For self-employed individuals and small business owners.
   - **Solo 401(k):** Another option for self-employed individuals with higher contribution limits.

Estimating Your Retirement Needs

To plan effectively, it's important to estimate how much money you'll need in retirement.

The Path to Financial Freedom: Mastering Money Management and Building Wealth

1. **Estimate Living Expenses:**
   Consider your lifestyle in retirement. Will your expenses be higher or lower than they are now? Don't forget healthcare costs, which can increase as you age.

2. **Use Retirement Calculators:**
   Online retirement calculators can help you estimate how much you need to save each month to reach your retirement goal. Consider factors such as inflation, investment returns, and how long you expect to live in retirement.

3. **Rule of Thumb:**
   A common rule of thumb is the **4% rule**, which suggests that you can withdraw 4% of your retirement savings annually without running out of money for at least 30 years.

Chapter 7: Diversifying Your Portfolio

The Importance of Asset Allocation

Asset allocation is the process of dividing your investments among different asset categories, such as stocks, bonds, and real estate. The goal is to reduce risk by spreading your investments across various asset classes.

1. **Diversification:**
   Diversifying your portfolio helps mitigate the risk of loss in any one investment. If one asset class underperforms, others may perform better, balancing out the overall performance of your portfolio.

2. **Risk Tolerance:**
   Your asset allocation should align with your risk tolerance and investment goals. Younger investors may choose a higher allocation to stocks for higher growth potential, while older investors may prefer bonds for stability.

How to Balance Risk and Reward

Balancing risk and reward is a critical aspect of investing. Here's how you can do it:

1. **Assess Your Risk Tolerance:**
   Risk tolerance varies from person to person. Some investors are comfortable with higher risk for higher returns, while others prefer stability. Understanding your risk tolerance helps you choose the right mix of assets.

2. **Adjust as You Age:**
   As you approach retirement, it's generally advisable to shift your portfolio toward more conservative investments (e.g., bonds) to protect your savings from market volatility.

Strategies for Long-Term Growth

1. **Buy and Hold:**
   A long-term investment strategy where you buy investments and hold them for an extended period, allowing them to grow over time.

2. **Rebalancing:**
   Periodically review your portfolio and adjust your asset allocation to maintain your desired risk level. This ensures that you're not overly exposed to any one asset class.

Chapter 8: Investing in Real Estate

Rental Properties, REITs, and House Hacking

Real estate can be a powerful way to build wealth, whether through direct ownership or investment in real estate-related assets.

1. **Rental Properties:**
   Owning rental properties allows you to generate passive income through rent payments. Over time, the property may also appreciate in value, providing a potential capital gain.

2. **REITs (Real Estate Investment Trusts):**
   REITs allow you to invest in real estate without directly owning property. These are companies that own or finance income-producing real estate and pay out dividends to shareholders.

3. **House Hacking:**
   House hacking involves purchasing a property, living in one part of it, and renting out the other part. This strategy can help you offset your mortgage payments and build equity.

Pros and Cons of Real Estate Investment

1. **Pros:**
    - Potential for high returns through rental income and property appreciation.
    - Tax advantages, such as deductions for mortgage interest and property depreciation.

- Real estate is a tangible asset that can act as a hedge against inflation.

2. **Cons:**
    - Requires significant upfront capital for purchasing properties.
    - Ongoing maintenance costs and property management responsibilities.
    - Real estate is illiquid, meaning it can take time to sell or access the value of the investment.

Steps to Get Started

1. **Research the Market:**
   Study local real estate markets to identify areas with potential for growth and good rental demand.

2. **Financing Options:**
   Explore different financing options, including traditional mortgages, FHA loans, or even real estate crowdfunding platforms.

3. **Start Small:**
   Begin with a small investment, such as a single-family home or a small rental property, and scale up as you gain experience.

Chapter 9: Navigating Cryptocurrency

What is Cryptocurrency?

Cryptocurrency is a form of digital or virtual currency that uses cryptography for security. The most popular

The Path to Financial Freedom: Mastering Money Management and Building Wealth

cryptocurrency is **Bitcoin**, but there are thousands of other digital currencies, such as **Ethereum** and **Litecoin**.

1. **Blockchain Technology:**
   Cryptocurrencies operate on a decentralized network called blockchain, which records all transactions transparently and securely.

Risks and Potential Rewards

1. **Risks:**
   - **Volatility:** Cryptocurrency prices are highly volatile, with significant price swings.
   - **Regulatory Uncertainty:** Governments around the world are still developing regulations for cryptocurrencies, which can affect their value and use.
   - **Security Risks:** While blockchain technology is secure, cryptocurrency exchanges and wallets can be vulnerable to hacking.

2. **Rewards:**
   - **High Returns:** Cryptocurrencies have the potential for significant returns, especially during periods of high demand.
   - **Diversification:** Adding cryptocurrency to your portfolio can provide diversification, as it behaves differently from traditional assets like stocks and bonds.

The Path to Financial Freedom: Mastering Money Management and Building Wealth

How to Invest Wisely in Digital Assets

1. **Do Your Research:**
   Thoroughly research each cryptocurrency before investing. Understand its use case, technology, and potential for long-term growth.

2. **Start Small:**
   Due to the volatility of the market, consider starting with a small percentage of your overall portfolio.

3. **Use Reputable Exchanges:**
   Choose well-known and reputable cryptocurrency exchanges to buy and store your digital assets securely.

Part 3: Creating Passive Income Streams

Chapter 10: The Concept of Passive Income

What It Is and Why It's Powerful

Passive income refers to income that requires little to no effort to earn and maintain. Unlike active income, where you trade time for money, passive income allows you to generate money with minimal ongoing effort once the initial work is done.

1. **The Power of Passive Income:**
   Passive income has the potential to provide financial freedom, as it allows you to earn money even when you're not actively working. It creates an opportunity for financial growth without the need for constant labor, freeing up your time to focus on other ventures or enjoy leisure activities.

The Path to Financial Freedom: Mastering Money Management and Building Wealth

2. **The Importance of Building Multiple Income Streams:**
   Relying solely on active income from a job or business can be risky. Building passive income streams diversifies your income sources, offering more stability and growth potential over time.

Active Income vs. Passive Income

1. **Active Income:**
   Active income is money earned through direct labor, such as a salary, hourly wage, or fees for services. The key characteristic of active income is that you must work to earn it, and the income stops when you stop working.

2. **Passive Income:**
   Passive income, on the other hand, requires an initial investment of time, money, or effort but can continue to generate income with minimal active involvement. Examples include rental income, dividends from stocks, or earnings from a blog or YouTube channel.

3. **The Transition to Passive Income:**
   While active income may be necessary in the early stages of your financial journey, shifting towards passive income is a key strategy for achieving long-term wealth and financial independence. Over time, passive income can grow and eventually surpass active income.

The Path to Financial Freedom: Mastering Money Management and Building Wealth

Chapter 11: Online Business Ventures

Blogging, eBooks, and Affiliate Marketing

1. **Blogging:**
   Blogging is a popular way to create passive income. By writing articles on topics you're passionate about or knowledgeable in, you can attract traffic to your website and monetize it through ads, affiliate links, or sponsored content.
   - **Monetizing Your Blog:**
     Once you have a steady stream of traffic, you can monetize your blog through Google AdSense, affiliate marketing, or selling your own products or services.

2. **eBooks:**
   Writing and selling eBooks is a great way to earn passive income. Once you've written and published your eBook, it can be sold on platforms like Amazon Kindle or your own website, generating income with minimal ongoing effort.
   - **Creating and Selling eBooks:**
     Focus on topics that have a demand, and ensure your book provides value to readers. Promote your eBook through social media, your blog, or email marketing to maximize sales.

3. **Affiliate Marketing:**
   Affiliate marketing involves promoting products or services from other companies and earning a commission for each sale made through your referral link. It's an effective way to generate

The Path to Financial Freedom: Mastering Money Management and Building Wealth

passive income, especially if you have a blog, YouTube channel, or social media following.

- o **Choosing Affiliate Products:**
  Select products or services that align with your audience's interests and needs. High-quality, relevant products will lead to higher conversion rates.

Starting a Dropshipping or E-Commerce Store

1. **Dropshipping:**
   Dropshipping allows you to sell products without holding inventory. When a customer places an order, the supplier ships the product directly to the customer. Your role is to market and sell the product, while the supplier handles fulfillment.

   - o **Pros of Dropshipping:**
     Low startup costs, no need for inventory management, and scalability. However, it's competitive, and profit margins can be thin.

2. **E-Commerce Store:**
   Running an e-commerce store involves selling physical or digital products directly to customers. Unlike dropshipping, you'll need to manage inventory, shipping, and customer service, but it offers higher control and potential for profit.

   - o **Setting Up an E-Commerce Store:**
     Use platforms like Shopify, WooCommerce, or BigCommerce to set up your store. Focus on building a strong brand, optimizing your product listings, and driving traffic through SEO and digital marketing.

The Path to Financial Freedom: Mastering Money Management and Building Wealth

Leveraging Social Media for Profit

1. **Building a Social Media Following:**
   Social media platforms like Instagram, YouTube, and TikTok can be powerful tools for building an audience and monetizing your content. Engage with your followers, share valuable content, and build trust to create opportunities for monetization.

2. **Monetizing Social Media:**
   Once you've built a following, you can monetize your social media presence through sponsored posts, affiliate marketing, selling your own products, or offering services like consulting or coaching.

Chapter 12: Investing in Dividend Stocks

How Dividends Work

Dividends are payments made by companies to their shareholders as a share of the company's profits. These payments are typically made on a quarterly basis and can be a reliable source of passive income.

1. **Dividend Yield:**
   The dividend yield is the annual dividend payment divided by the stock price. A higher dividend yield can provide more income, but it's important to assess the sustainability of the dividend before investing.

2. **Dividend Growth:**
   Companies that consistently increase their dividends over time are considered good

investments for those seeking long-term passive income. Reinvesting dividends can further accelerate wealth accumulation.

Building a Portfolio of Dividend-Paying Stocks

1. **Selecting Dividend Stocks:**
   Choose companies with a history of paying reliable and increasing dividends. Focus on well-established companies in stable industries, such as utilities, consumer goods, or healthcare.

2. **Diversification:**
   Diversify your dividend stock portfolio to spread risk. Invest in companies across different sectors to reduce the impact of market fluctuations on your overall portfolio.

3. **Reinvesting Dividends for Growth:**
   Instead of cashing out dividends, reinvest them back into more shares of the stock. This strategy allows your investment to compound over time, leading to exponential growth.

Chapter 13: Peer-to-Peer Lending and Crowdfunding

How Peer-to-Peer (P2P) Lending Works

Peer-to-peer lending allows individuals to lend money to others through online platforms, bypassing traditional financial institutions. Lenders earn interest on the loans they provide, making it a potential source of passive income.

1. **P2P Lending Platforms:**
   Platforms like LendingClub, Prosper, and Funding

Circle connect borrowers with investors. As a lender, you can choose the loans you want to fund based on risk, return, and loan duration.

2. **Loan Terms and Interest Rates:**
   The interest rate on P2P loans is determined by the borrower's creditworthiness and the platform's policies. As a lender, you earn interest payments on the loan, typically monthly or quarterly.

Risks and Returns

1. **Risks:**
   P2P lending carries risks, including borrower default, platform failure, and liquidity issues. It's important to diversify your loans and assess the borrower's creditworthiness before lending.

2. **Returns:**
   P2P lending can offer attractive returns, often higher than traditional savings accounts or bonds. However, the risk of default means that returns are not guaranteed.

Platforms to Consider

1. **LendingClub:**
   LendingClub is one of the largest P2P lending platforms, offering personal loans, small business loans, and auto refinancing options.

2. **Prosper:**
   Prosper is another popular platform for personal loans, allowing investors to lend money to individuals with varying credit profiles.

3. **Funding Circle:**
   Funding Circle specializes in small business loans, allowing investors to lend money to growing businesses.

Chapter 14: Monetizing Your Skills

Creating Online Courses

1. **Why Create Online Courses:**
   If you have expertise in a particular field, creating an online course can be a great way to generate passive income. Platforms like Udemy, Teachable, and Skillshare make it easy to create, market, and sell courses.

2. **Course Creation Tips:**
   Focus on creating high-quality, valuable content that addresses the needs of your target audience. Use video, quizzes, and assignments to enhance the learning experience.

3. **Marketing Your Course:**
   Promote your course through social media, email marketing, and collaborations with influencers or bloggers in your niche.

Freelancing and Consulting

1. **Freelancing:**
   Freelancing allows you to monetize your skills by offering services like writing, graphic design, web development, or digital marketing. Platforms like Upwork, Fiverr, and Freelancer connect freelancers with clients.

2. **Consulting:**
   If you have significant expertise in a particular industry, consider offering consulting services. You can charge hourly rates or offer packaged services to help businesses solve specific problems.

Turning Hobbies into Income Streams

1. **Monetizing Hobbies:**
   Many people turn hobbies like photography, crafting, or gaming into income streams. Whether it's selling handmade goods on Etsy, offering photography services, or streaming on Twitch, your passion can become a profitable business.

2. **Building an Audience:**
   Use social media and online platforms to build an audience around your hobby. Engage with your followers, offer valuable content, and monetize your skills through product sales, services, or affiliate marketing.

Part 4: Achieving Financial Independence

Chapter 15: The FIRE Movement

What is Financial Independence, Retire Early (FIRE)?

The FIRE movement is a lifestyle philosophy that emphasizes achieving financial independence as early as possible, allowing individuals to retire or pursue their passions long before the traditional retirement age. The goal is to accumulate enough wealth and passive income streams to cover living expenses without needing to work.

The Path to Financial Freedom: Mastering Money Management and Building Wealth

1. **Core Principles of FIRE:**
    - **Financial Independence:** Accumulating enough assets to live off of without working.
    - **Retire Early:** The option to retire early or transition to work that is more fulfilling and less financially driven.
2. **The Importance of Financial Freedom:**
Achieving FIRE allows for greater freedom in how you spend your time, as you no longer have to rely on a traditional paycheck. This can lead to a more fulfilling life, whether you choose to pursue hobbies, travel, or work on passion projects.

Different Types of FIRE: Lean, Fat, and Barista

1. **Lean FIRE:**
Lean FIRE is achieved by living extremely frugally and cutting expenses to the bare minimum. Individuals who pursue Lean FIRE typically aim to live on a modest budget, often well below the average cost of living.
2. **Fat FIRE:**
Fat FIRE is the pursuit of financial independence with a higher standard of living. Those who follow Fat FIRE aim to save more aggressively, allowing for a more comfortable lifestyle in retirement, including luxuries like travel, fine dining, and other discretionary spending.
3. **Barista FIRE:**
Barista FIRE is a hybrid approach where individuals achieve partial financial independence and can choose to work part-time or in a less

demanding job. The goal is to reduce the number of hours worked while still having enough savings and investments to cover living expenses.

Steps to Achieve FIRE

1. **Assess Your Current Financial Situation:**
   - Calculate your net worth, income, and expenses.
   - Identify areas where you can cut costs and increase savings.

2. **Increase Your Income:**
   - Pursue side hustles, negotiate salary increases, or develop additional income streams like passive income.

3. **Aggressive Saving and Investing:**
   - Save a significant portion of your income (50% or more is common in the FIRE community).
   - Invest in low-cost index funds, stocks, bonds, or real estate to grow your wealth.

4. **Minimize Expenses:**
   - Adopt frugal living habits to reduce unnecessary spending and maximize savings.

5. **Monitor Progress:**
   - Regularly track your financial goals and adjust your strategy as needed.

The Path to Financial Freedom: Mastering Money Management and Building Wealth

Chapter 16: Tax Optimization Strategies

Understanding Tax Brackets and Deductions

1. **Tax Brackets:**
   Tax brackets are the ranges of income that are taxed at different rates. Understanding where your income falls within these brackets can help you minimize taxes and maximize your savings.

   - **Progressive Tax System:**
     Most countries, including the U.S., use a progressive tax system where the more you earn, the higher your tax rate on that income. Being aware of this system helps you make smarter financial decisions.

2. **Tax Deductions:**
   Tax deductions reduce your taxable income, lowering the amount of taxes you owe. Common deductions include mortgage interest, student loan interest, and charitable contributions.

   - **Standard vs. Itemized Deductions:**
     Choose between the standard deduction or itemizing deductions based on which option offers the greater tax savings.

Tax-Advantaged Accounts

1. **Retirement Accounts:**
   Tax-advantaged accounts like 401(k)s, IRAs, and Roth IRAs allow you to save for retirement while reducing your current tax liability.

- **Traditional 401(k) and IRA:**
  Contributions are tax-deductible, and taxes are paid when you withdraw funds in retirement.
- **Roth IRA:**
  Contributions are made with after-tax dollars, but withdrawals in retirement are tax-free.

2. **Health Savings Accounts (HSAs):**
   HSAs are a tax-advantaged way to save for medical expenses. Contributions are tax-deductible, and withdrawals for qualified medical expenses are tax-free.

3. **529 College Savings Plans:**
   If you have children or plan to pay for higher education, 529 plans offer tax-free growth for educational expenses.

Reducing Your Tax Burden Legally

1. **Maximize Retirement Contributions:**
   Contribute the maximum allowable amount to tax-advantaged retirement accounts, reducing your taxable income in the process.

2. **Capital Gains Tax Optimization:**
   If you invest in stocks, real estate, or other assets, be mindful of capital gains taxes. Holding investments for over a year allows you to benefit from lower long-term capital gains tax rates.

3. **Tax-Loss Harvesting:**
   Offset gains by selling losing investments to reduce

The Path to Financial Freedom: Mastering Money Management and Building Wealth

your taxable income. This strategy helps you minimize taxes on investment returns.

4. **Charitable Giving:**
   Donating to charity can reduce your taxable income. Donations to qualified organizations are deductible, and you can use this strategy to both reduce taxes and support causes you care about.

Chapter 17: Frugality and Mindful Spending

Living Below Your Means

1. **The Importance of Frugality:**
   Living below your means is one of the most effective ways to build wealth. By spending less than you earn, you can save and invest more, accelerating your path to financial independence.

2. **Creating a Budget:**
   Set a realistic budget that reflects your income, expenses, and savings goals. Track your spending to ensure you're living within your means and avoid overspending.

3. **The Power of Automating Savings:**
   Automate your savings and investment contributions to ensure you consistently save a portion of your income before you have a chance to spend it.

The Difference Between Needs and Wants

1. **Needs vs. Wants:**
   Needs are essential for survival, such as food, shelter, and healthcare. Wants are non-essential

items that enhance your lifestyle but aren't necessary for basic living.

2. **Cutting Back on Wants:**
Identifying and eliminating unnecessary wants can free up more money for savings and investments. Practice mindful spending by focusing on what truly adds value to your life.

3. **Making Conscious Spending Decisions:**
Evaluate purchases based on their long-term value and impact on your financial goals. Consider alternatives to expensive items, such as secondhand goods or DIY solutions.

Finding Joy in Simplicity

1. **Minimalism and Financial Independence:**
Embracing minimalism can lead to greater financial freedom. By reducing material possessions and simplifying your lifestyle, you can focus on what truly matters and save more money.

2. **Enjoying Life Without Excess:**
You don't need to spend a lot of money to enjoy life. Find joy in simple experiences like spending time with family, exploring nature, or learning new skills.

Chapter 18: Staying Motivated on Your Financial Journey

Tracking Progress Toward Goals

1. **Setting SMART Goals:**
Set specific, measurable, achievable, relevant, and time-bound (SMART) goals for your financial

journey. Break down long-term goals into smaller, manageable milestones.

2. **Monitoring Financial Progress:**
   Use tools like budgeting apps, spreadsheets, or financial software to track your income, expenses, savings, and investments. Regularly review your progress to stay on track.

Dealing with Setbacks

1. **Staying Resilient:**
   Financial setbacks are inevitable, whether it's an unexpected expense, market downturn, or personal crisis. The key is to stay resilient and adjust your plan when necessary.

2. **Learning from Mistakes:**
   Mistakes are a part of the journey. Use setbacks as learning experiences to refine your financial strategy and avoid making the same errors in the future.

Celebrating Milestones

1. **Recognizing Achievements:**
   Celebrate your progress along the way, whether it's paying off debt, reaching a savings goal, or achieving financial independence. Acknowledging milestones helps maintain motivation and reinforces positive financial habits.

2. **Rewarding Yourself Responsibly:**
   While it's important to stay focused on your long-term goals, it's also essential to reward yourself for your hard work. Treat yourself to small rewards that

align with your values and don't derail your financial progress.

Conclusion and Next Steps

Recap of Key Takeaways

As you reach the end of this book, you now have a solid understanding of the essential strategies to manage your finances, grow your wealth, and achieve financial independence. Let's recap the key takeaways:

1. **Building a Strong Financial Foundation**

    o Understanding your financial health is the first step. Assessing your income, expenses, and debts helps you determine where you stand financially and sets the stage for your financial goals.

    o Budgeting is critical for ensuring that your spending aligns with your priorities. Whether you follow the 50/30/20 rule or another method, tracking your expenses is the key to financial control.

    o Eliminating debt should be a priority. By tackling high-interest debt first and using strategies like the snowball or avalanche methods, you can free up more money for savings and investing.

    o Building an emergency fund is essential for financial security. It acts as a safety net, giving you peace of mind in case of unexpected expenses or financial setbacks.

The Path to Financial Freedom: Mastering Money Management and Building Wealth

2. **Growing Your Wealth Through Smart Investing**

    o   Investing is the key to growing your wealth over time. Understanding different investment vehicles like stocks, bonds, mutual funds, and ETFs helps you make informed decisions that align with your risk tolerance and financial goals.

    o   Retirement planning is crucial for long-term financial security. By contributing to tax-advantaged accounts like 401(k)s and IRAs, you ensure that you have enough to retire comfortably.

    o   Diversifying your portfolio spreads risk and increases your chances of long-term growth. Balancing assets like stocks, bonds, and real estate ensures that you are not overly reliant on any one investment.

    o   Real estate can be a powerful wealth-building tool, whether through rental properties, REITs, or house hacking. It provides an opportunity for both passive income and long-term appreciation.

    o   Cryptocurrency offers potential for growth, but it comes with high risk. Understanding the fundamentals of digital assets and investing wisely is key to navigating this emerging market.

3. **Creating Passive Income Streams**

- Passive income is a powerful tool for achieving financial independence. By investing in assets that generate income without active involvement, you can build wealth over time while freeing up your time for other pursuits.
- Online business ventures, such as blogging, eBooks, and affiliate marketing, allow you to leverage your skills and interests to generate income. Starting an e-commerce store or dropshipping business can also provide a scalable way to earn money online.
- Dividend stocks offer a reliable income stream, and reinvesting dividends can accelerate the growth of your wealth.
- Peer-to-peer lending and crowdfunding platforms allow you to earn interest by lending money to individuals or funding projects. These platforms offer an alternative to traditional investments with the potential for high returns.
- Monetizing your skills through freelancing, consulting, or creating online courses can provide a flexible and rewarding way to generate income.

4. **Achieving Financial Independence**
   - The FIRE movement provides a roadmap for those who want to retire early or gain financial independence. By aggressively

The Path to Financial Freedom: Mastering Money Management and Building Wealth

    saving and investing, you can build enough wealth to live on your terms.

- Tax optimization strategies, such as contributing to tax-advantaged accounts and minimizing capital gains taxes, help you keep more of your hard-earned money.

- Frugality and mindful spending are essential for living below your means and accelerating your path to financial independence. By distinguishing between needs and wants, you can prioritize saving and investing.

- Staying motivated on your financial journey is key to success. Tracking progress, dealing with setbacks, and celebrating milestones keep you focused and energized as you move toward your financial goals.

How to Start Implementing Strategies Today

Now that you have the knowledge and tools to take control of your finances, it's time to start implementing these strategies. Here's how you can take action today:

1. **Assess Your Financial Health**
   - Begin by evaluating your current financial situation. Calculate your net worth, track your expenses, and identify any high-interest debt. This will give you a clear picture of where you stand and help you set realistic financial goals.

- Use budgeting tools or apps like Mint, YNAB (You Need a Budget), or a simple spreadsheet to track your income and expenses. This will help you stay on top of your finances and ensure that you're living within your means.

2. **Create a Budget**
    - Choose a budgeting method that works for you. Whether you prefer the 50/30/20 rule or another approach, start by allocating your income to essentials, savings, and discretionary spending. Stick to your budget and adjust it as needed to stay on track.

3. **Eliminate Debt**
    - If you have outstanding debt, prioritize paying it off. Use the snowball or avalanche method to focus on either the smallest debts or the highest-interest debts first. Consider consolidating or refinancing your loans to reduce interest rates and accelerate repayment.

4. **Start Investing**
    - Open a retirement account like a 401(k) or IRA if you haven't already. Contribute as much as you can, especially if your employer offers matching contributions.
    - Start investing in low-cost index funds or ETFs to build a diversified portfolio. Consider working with a financial advisor if

The Path to Financial Freedom: Mastering Money Management and Building Wealth

you need help choosing investments that align with your risk tolerance and financial goals.

- o If you're interested in real estate, start by researching local markets, rental properties, or REITs. Look into platforms like Fundrise or RealtyMogul to get started with real estate investments.

5. **Build Passive Income Streams**

    - o Identify opportunities for passive income that align with your skills and interests. Start by creating a blog, writing an eBook, or exploring affiliate marketing. Consider launching an online business or investing in dividend stocks to generate passive income over time.

    - o Research platforms for peer-to-peer lending and crowdfunding if you're interested in these alternative investment options. Make sure to understand the risks and potential returns before diving in.

6. **Adopt Frugal Habits**

    - o Review your spending habits and identify areas where you can cut back. Focus on needs rather than wants, and find joy in simplicity. Automate your savings and investments to ensure that you're consistently building wealth.

7. **Set Financial Goals**

The Path to Financial Freedom: Mastering Money Management and Building Wealth

- Set SMART (Specific, Measurable, Achievable, Relevant, Time-bound) financial goals. Break them down into smaller milestones and track your progress regularly. This will keep you motivated and focused on your financial journey.

Encouragement for the Journey Ahead

Embarking on the path to financial independence is a journey that requires patience, discipline, and persistence. While the road may be challenging at times, the rewards are worth the effort. Remember, financial freedom doesn't happen overnight—it's the result of consistent, smart decisions over time.

Stay committed to your goals, and don't be discouraged by setbacks. Every step you take brings you closer to achieving financial independence. Whether you're just starting or are already on your way, know that you have the power to create the life you desire.

Celebrate your progress, learn from your mistakes, and keep moving forward. With the knowledge and strategies you've gained from this book, you are well-equipped to take control of your finances and achieve the financial freedom you deserve.

Good luck on your journey, and remember that financial independence is not just a destination, it's a lifestyle. You have the tools, the knowledge, and the determination to make it a reality. Keep pushing forward and enjoy the journey ahead!

The Path to Financial Freedom: Mastering Money Management and Building Wealth

Appendices and Resources

Glossary of Financial Terms

Understanding financial terminology is crucial to making informed decisions and managing your money effectively. Below is a glossary of essential financial terms you may encounter as you continue your financial journey:

1. Asset
An asset is anything of value or a resource that can be converted into cash. Common assets include cash, real estate, stocks, bonds, and personal property.

2. Budgeting
Budgeting is the process of creating a plan to manage your income and expenses. It helps ensure that you live within your means and save for future goals.

3. Compound Interest
Compound interest refers to interest that is calculated on both the initial principal and the accumulated interest from previous periods. It accelerates the growth of your investments over time.

4. Credit Score
A credit score is a numerical representation of your creditworthiness, typically ranging from 300 to 850. It is used by lenders to assess the risk of lending to you.

5. Debt-to-Income Ratio (DTI)
This ratio measures the percentage of your monthly income that goes toward paying debts. A lower DTI indicates better financial health and is often required for loan approval.

6. Diversification
Diversification is an investment strategy that involves

spreading your investments across various assets to reduce risk. A diversified portfolio may include stocks, bonds, real estate, and other asset types.

7. Emergency Fund

An emergency fund is a savings reserve set aside for unexpected expenses, such as medical bills, car repairs, or job loss. Financial experts recommend having three to six months' worth of living expenses saved in an emergency fund.

8. Equity

Equity refers to the value of an asset after subtracting any liabilities or debts associated with it. For example, the equity in your home is the difference between its market value and the mortgage balance.

9. ETF (Exchange-Traded Fund)

An ETF is a type of investment fund that holds a collection of assets, such as stocks or bonds. It is traded on stock exchanges, similar to individual stocks, and offers a cost-effective way to diversify your portfolio.

10. Financial Independence

Financial independence means having enough wealth and passive income to cover your living expenses without needing to work for a paycheck. It is the ultimate goal of the FIRE movement.

11. FIRE (Financial Independence, Retire Early)

FIRE is a movement focused on achieving financial independence and retiring early. It involves aggressively saving and investing to build wealth quickly and live off passive income.

The Path to Financial Freedom: Mastering Money Management and Building Wealth

12. Fixed Expenses
Fixed expenses are regular, predictable costs that do not change from month to month, such as rent or mortgage payments, utilities, and insurance premiums.

13. Frugality
Frugality is the practice of being mindful of your spending and making intentional choices to live below your means. It involves prioritizing needs over wants and finding value in everyday purchases.

14. Index Fund
An index fund is a type of mutual fund or ETF that aims to replicate the performance of a specific market index, such as the S&P 500. It is a low-cost, passive investment strategy.

15. Investment Portfolio
An investment portfolio is a collection of financial assets, such as stocks, bonds, and real estate, held by an individual or institution. The goal of a portfolio is to achieve a balance of risk and return based on the investor's financial goals.

16. Liability
A liability is a financial obligation or debt that you owe to another party, such as credit card balances, student loans, or mortgages.

17. Net Worth
Net worth is the difference between your total assets and your total liabilities. It is a measure of your financial health and reflects the value of what you own versus what you owe.

18. Passive Income
Passive income is money earned with minimal effort or

active involvement. It typically comes from investments, rental properties, royalties, or business ventures that require little ongoing work.

19. Portfolio Diversification
Portfolio diversification is the strategy of spreading your investments across various asset classes to reduce risk. This approach aims to ensure that a decline in one investment doesn't significantly impact the entire portfolio.

20. REIT (Real Estate Investment Trust)
A REIT is a company that owns, operates, or finances income-producing real estate. REITs allow investors to pool their money to invest in large-scale real estate projects without directly owning property.

21. Risk Tolerance
Risk tolerance is the level of risk an investor is willing to take on in their investment portfolio. It is influenced by factors such as age, financial goals, and personal comfort with market fluctuations.

22. Roth IRA
A Roth IRA (Individual Retirement Account) is a retirement account that allows you to invest after-tax money. The benefit is that qualified withdrawals are tax-free in retirement.

23. Stock
A stock represents ownership in a company. When you buy stock, you are purchasing a small piece of the company and may benefit from its profits in the form of dividends or capital appreciation.

24. Tax-Advantaged Accounts
Tax-advantaged accounts are investment accounts that

The Path to Financial Freedom: Mastering Money Management and Building Wealth

provide tax benefits, such as tax-deferred growth or tax-free withdrawals. Examples include 401(k)s, IRAs, and HSAs (Health Savings Accounts).

25. Time Value of Money
The time value of money is the concept that money today is worth more than the same amount in the future due to its potential to earn interest or generate returns. This principle is fundamental to investing and wealth-building strategies.

26. Wealth Building
Wealth building is the process of accumulating assets and increasing net worth over time. It involves earning, saving, and investing money in ways that grow your financial resources.

www.ingramcontent.com/pod-product-compliance
Lightning Source LLC
Chambersburg PA
CBHW030054230526
45471CB00003B/1090